NATURAL MARVELS

Treasures of
the Oceans

WORLD
BOOK

World Book, Inc.
180 North LaSalle Street, Suite 900
Chicago, Illinois 60601
USA

For information about other World Book publications, please visit our website at www.worldbook.com or call 1-800-WORLDBK (967-5325).

For information about sales to schools and libraries, please call 1-800-975-3250 (United States) or 1-800-837-5365 (Canada).

Library of Congress Cataloging-in-Publication Data

Title: Treasures of the oceans.
Description: Chicago, Illinois: World Book, Inc., a Scott Fetzer Company, [2017] | Series: Natural marvels | Includes index.
Identifiers: LCCN 2016052010 | ISBN 9780716633709
Subjects: LCSH: Ocean--Juvenile literature. | Great Barrier Reef (Qld.)--Juvenile literature. | Coral reefs and islands--Maldives--Juvenile literature. | Mid-Atlantic Ridge--Juvenile literature.
Classification: LCC GC21.5 .T74 2017 | DDC 551.46/8--dc23
LC record available at https://lccn.loc.gov/2016052010

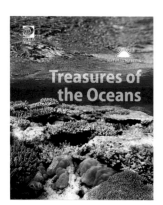

Over eons, the forces of nature have sculpted Earth in certain locations to create majestic landscapes of great beauty. Some of the most spectacular landforms are featured in this series of books. This image shows the Great Barrier Reef off the coast of Australia.

This edition:
ISBN: 978-0-7166-3370-9 (hc.)
ISBN: 978-0-7166-3363-1 (set, hc.)

Also available as:
ISBN: 978-0-7166-3379-2
(e-book, EPUB3)

Printed in China by Shenzhen Wing King Tong Paper Products Co., Ltd. Shenzhen, Guangdong
1st printing March 2017

Table of Contents

Glossary There is a glossary of terms on page 38. Terms defined in the glossary are in type **that looks like this** on their first appearance on any spread (two facing pages). Words that are difficult to say are followed by a pronunciation (*pruh NUHN see AY shuhn*) the first time they are mentioned.

Introduction

Ancient people feared the sea, and not without reason. The ocean is hostile to human life. We cannot drink the ocean's salty water, let alone breathe in it. Throughout the ages, countless ships have been lost at sea, wrecked by storms, or smashed against underwater rock formations called **reefs.**

And yet people have always been drawn to the ocean's mysteries. The ocean covers 70 percent of Earth's surface. Its floor is mostly hidden from our view. Even with all of our modern technology, we've seen far less of the ocean bottom than the surface of the moon. What treasures lie beneath the waves?

This book explores three spectacular places hidden in the ocean. The first, the Great Barrier Reef, stretches for 1,400 miles (2,300 kilometers) just off Australia's northeast coast. This vast structure, visible from the moon, is built entirely from the skeletons of jellyfishlike creatures—**corals.**

Another group of ring-shaped coral reefs, the **Atolls** of the Maldives, form hundreds of islands in the tropical waters of the Indian Ocean. The platforms for these rings of coral are the slopes of underwater volcanoes.

A third ocean marvel, the Mid-Atlantic Ridge, is a vast chain of underwater volcanoes. It rises from a gash in Earth's crust that runs about 10,000 miles (16,000 kilometers) down the entire Atlantic Ocean.

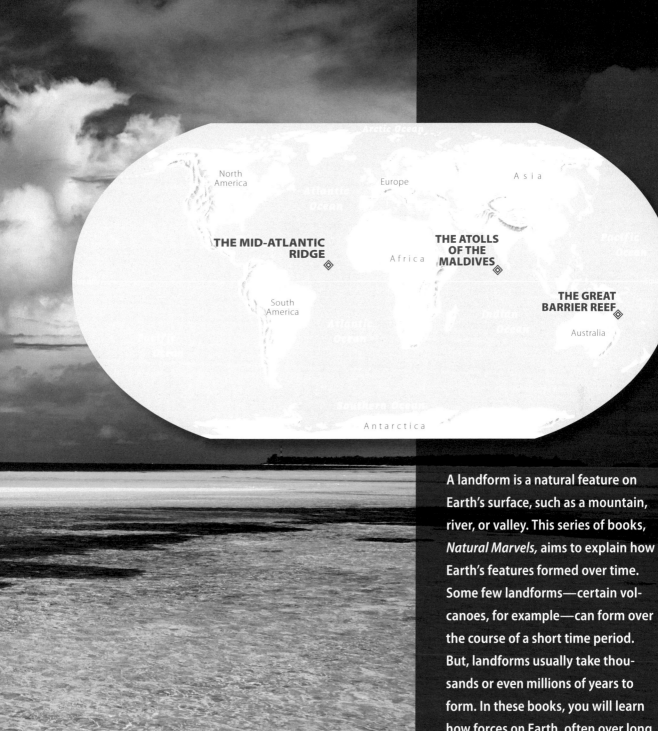

Arctic Ocean

North
America

Europe

Asia

Atlantic
Ocean

**THE MID-ATLANTIC
RIGE** ◈

Africa

**THE ATOLLS
OF THE
MALDIVES** ◈

Pacific
Ocean

South
America

Atlantic
Ocean

**THE GREAT
BARRIER REEF** ◈

Australia

Pacific
Ocean

Indian
Ocean

Southern Ocean

Antarctica

A landform is a natural feature on Earth's surface, such as a mountain, river, or valley. This series of books, *Natural Marvels,* aims to explain how Earth's features formed over time. Some few landforms—certain volcanoes, for example—can form over the course of a short time period. But, landforms usually take thousands or even millions of years to form. In these books, you will learn how forces on Earth, often over long time periods, can create landscapes of great beauty.

The Great Barrier Reef

Where Is the Great Barrier Reef and What's Special About It?

The Great Barrier Reef is the largest chain of coral **reefs** in the world. It is made of about 3,000 individual reefs. Together, they act like a barrier between Australia's coast and the open ocean beyond.

The reefs form a gigantic underwater city. Their nooks and crannies provide shelter to countless fish, crabs, shrimp, sea stars, mollusks, and, of course, **corals.** Many of these creatures flash with brilliant colors in the reef's crystal-clear water.

Like human cities, the Great Barrier Reef is full of variety. Coral reefs are rich in **biodiversity.** More kinds of living things make their home in the Great Barrier Reef than almost anywhere else on Earth. Because of its size, beauty, and variety of life, the Great Barrier Reef is often listed as one of the "seven natural wonders of the world."

The Great Barrier Reef along the northeast coast of Australia is the world's largest group of coral reefs, famous for its beauty and for the variety of its wildlife.

Gulf of Papua

PAPUA
NEW GUINEA

Port
Moresby

Torres
Strait

Murray Is.

Providential
Channel

GREAT BARRIER REEF

South Pacific
Ocean

N

Coral Sea

Lizard I.

Cooktown

Endeavour Reef

Green I.

Cairns

Dunk I.

Bedarra I.

Hinchinbrook I.

Orpheus I.

Magnetic I.

Townsville

Queensland

South Molle I.

Daydream I.

Long I.

Newry I.

Mackay

Hayman I.

Whitsunday I.

Lindeman I.

Brampton I.

Swain
Reefs

AUSTRALIA

Capricorn Channel

Rockhampton

Great Keppel I.

Heron I.

Gladstone

Quoin I.

Bundaberg

◆ Point of interest

● City or town

0   100   200 Miles

0   100   200   300 Kilometers

What Creature Built the Great Barrier Reef?

Corals are ocean animals related to jellyfish and sea anemones (*uh NEHM uh neez*). Like their relatives, corals have many sharp, painful stingers—so other animals are not tempted to eat them. An individual coral takes the form of a wormlike **polyp** (*POL ihp*). A polyp stays rooted to one place. To eat, a polyp wiggles its tentacles, drawing in bits of food from the water.

Corals don't look like they'd be great architects. Yet these tiny, brainless animals built the whole Great Barrier Reef. In fact, all coral **reefs** are built by a type of coral called stony corals. What's their secret?

Stony corals have a few secrets up their sleeves (or polyps). The first secret is **limestone.** When corals suck in seawater, they also suck in calcium, a mineral dissolved in seawater. Inside corals, this calcium changes to form calcium carbonate—the main ingredient in limestone rock. Over time, coral polyps leave a limestone "skeleton" around their bodies. This limestone usually grows about 5 inches (13 centimeters) per year. Over millions of years, the skeletons of corals built up, and up, and up— forming the Great Barrier Reef and other reefs.

Another coral secret: they work together. Corals grow in **colonies.** Much like an ant colony, or a human city, a coral colony shares food and resources among its many polyps. In some ways, a coral reef works more like a single, enormous living thing than a collection of individual animals.

Most reef-building coral animals, also known as stony corals, live together in colonies. Corals produce formations that may look like branching trees, large domes, small irregular crusts, or tiny organ pipes.

11

The Secret of Symbiosis

Corals have another secret. They don't just share food and resources with other corals. A coral shares its own body with an entirely different kind of living thing: **zooxanthellae** (*zoh uh zan thel ee*), a type of **algae** (*AL jee*). This relationship between corals and zooxanthellae makes coral reefs so full of life.

Most life on Earth depends on sunlight. Plants on Earth's dry surface make food from sunlight, a process called **photosynthesis.** In the ocean, plantlike algae do the same thing. Animals, in turn, eat plants and algae. But plants and algae need more than just sunlight. They also need **nutrients**— minerals and other substances dissolved in water.

The bright, clear waters of the Great Barrier Reef get plenty of sunlight. But they do not actually contain much dissolved nutrients. How, then, can the reef support such an explosion of life?

The answer lies with corals and zooxanthellae. Like other algae, zooxanthellae use the sun's energy to make food. They share some food with their coral host and help it build limestone. The coral, in turn, provides the algae with some of the nutrients they need. Corals also protect zooxanthellae from being eaten—coral polyps, with their sharp stingers, make for a painful meal. The relationship between corals and zooxanthellae, called **symbiosis** (*sihm by OH sihs or sihm bee OH sihs*), is good for both animals. Working together, they make the most out of their nutrient-poor tropical waters.

ANOTHER OCEAN WONDER

Of the "seven natural wonders," the Great Barrier Reef is one of only two that lie in the ocean. The other is the harbor of Rio de Janeiro. This beautiful bay in Brazil is surrounded by mountains and studded with islands. When Portuguese sailors found the bay in the early 1500's, they thought—wrongly—that it was the mouth of a great river, so they called it the River of January, or Rio de Janeiro in Portuguese.

Coral reefs contain an amazing diversity of life made possible by the relationship between corals and zooxanthellae.

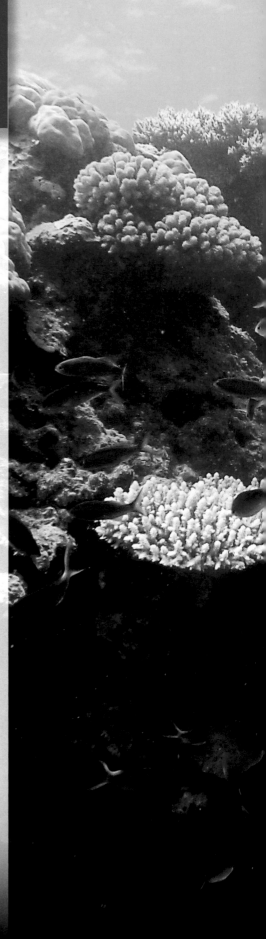

The Rain Forest of the Ocean

Like a city, the Great Barrier Reef is crowded. More kinds of creatures live in and around its **limestone** "buildings" than almost anywhere else on Earth. Only rain forests have more **biodiversity** than coral reefs. For this reason, coral reefs are often called the "rain forests of the oceans."

Huge numbers of fish live in the Great Barrier Reef. They come in every color of the rainbow. Their shapes and sizes are just as varied. Many are specially **adapted** for life amongst corals. Parrotfish, for example, have beaklike front teeth. They use these teeth to scrape **algae** off limestone. Other fish are a bit more dangerous. Moray eels look more like snakes than fish. Their body shape lets them easily hide in the nooks and crannies of the reefs and then dart out to catch other fish to eat. Many kinds of sharks and rays hunt in the Great Barrier Reef.

Sea turtle

The Great Barrier Reef is also home to reptiles. They include several kinds of sea turtles and some of the most poisonous sea snakes in the world. Dolphins and whales also visit the Great Barrier Reef.

A blue starfish, also called a sea star (above left), makes its way across a coral, while a jellyfish (above) swims slowly past the Great Barrier Reef.

Fish, reptiles, dolphins, and whales all have backbones. Most of the creatures that live in the Great Barrier Reef, however, do not. They are **invertebrates (**ihn VUR tuh brihtz**).** Such creatures include shrimp and crabs, with hard shells instead of internal skeletons. Clams, snails, squids, and octopuses are invertebrates, too. The giant clam, the largest clam in the world, lives in the Great Barrier Reef.

A red octopus (below) is one of the larger invertebrates that makes its home at the Great Barrier Reef.

Other reef invertebrates include many kinds of sea stars and sea urchins. Jellyfish and flowerlike sea anemones are invertebrates, too. And the most important invertebrate of all is, of course, the coral!

15

All Together Now

Corals are not the only reef creatures to have a symbiotic relationship with **zooxanthellae.** The **algae** also live in giant clams. They lend the clam's flesh its brilliant colors.

Other reef creatures have **symbiotic** relationships with each other. The wrasse is a small, colorful fish that often swims alongside larger fish. Wrasses eat tiny creatures attached to a larger fish's body. The wrasse gets a free meal, and the big fish gets a free cleaning!

The clownfish (also called the anemonefish) has a symbiotic relationship with sea anemones. Anemones, like corals and jellyfish, have stinging tentacles. These stingers hurt most fish, but not the clownfish. The clownfish hides in the anemone's waving tentacles, keeping safe from larger fish. In turn, the clownfish eats smaller creatures that might harm the anemone.

The brilliant colors of the giant clam (above) are due to zooxan-thellae living inside it.

STAR OF DESTRUCTION

While most of the creatures in the Great Barrier Reef live in balance with one another, there is one big exception. One of the few animals that eats coral polyps, the foundation of the whole reef system, is the adult crown of thorns sea star. Even a handful of these sea stars can strip huge areas of corals.

A crown of thorns (above) slowly makes a meal of a coral at the Great Barrier Reef.

A clownfish (above left) shelters in the tentacles of an anemone, while a red coral trout gets a cleaning from a small blue wrasse (left).

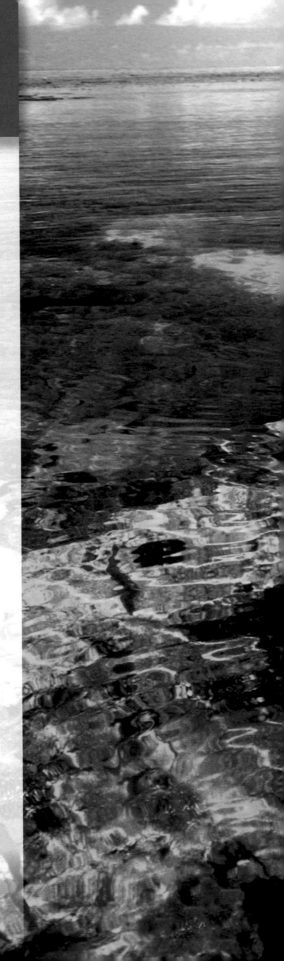

The Great Barrier Reef and People

Many people visit the Great Barrier Reef for sight-seeing and scuba diving. Other activities are strictly controlled. The Great Barrier Reef Marine Park Authority (an agency created by the governments of Australia and Queensland) is in charge of protecting the reef. Even so, human activities threaten the Great Barrier Reef.

Reefs have long been hazards for ships, and the Great Barrier Reef is no exception. But today's gigantic ships can cause much damage to a coral reef. They may also leak oil, chemicals, or other harmful materials into the water.

Some scientists believe human activity is responsible for a major threat to the reef: the crown of thorns sea star. Farmers often use chemicals that supply extra **nutrients** to crops. These chemicals may run off from farms and wash into the ocean, near the Great Barrier Reef. This runoff provides nutrients to tiny organisms eaten by young sea stars, so more survive to adulthood. More adult crown of thorns, in turn, mean more dead corals.

Global warming, the observed rise in Earth's average surface temperature, may be the biggest threat to the reef. Scientists believe global warming is caused by human activity, especially burning fuel in cars and power plants. In the past decades, Earth's oceans have warmed. If the water gets too warm, **zooxanthellae** leave the bodies of corals. The corals became pale and soon die off, a process called *coral bleaching.*

A swimmer uses a short breathing tube called a snorkel to view colorful corals underwater at the Great Barrier Reef.

The Atolls of the Maldives

Where Are the Atolls of the Maldives and What's Special About Them?

When you imagine a tropical island paradise, you might picture an **atoll.** An atoll is a ring-shaped coral reef in the open sea. Atolls form flat islands. Their land is covered with tropical grass and coconut palms. Beautiful sandy beaches fringe the shores. In the center of an atoll, you might see a clear, shallow pool of water called a lagoon.

The Maldives is a country in the Indian Ocean made entirely of atolls. It is a chain of about 1,200 tiny islands, 475 miles (74 kilometers) long— roughly the length of the U.S. state of Florida. None of the islands covers more than 5 square miles (13 square kilometers). Most are much smaller. The islands barely rise above sea level. In fact, the Maldives is the lowest country in the world.

Now, coral reefs do not just float on the open ocean, like rafts. **Limestone** is heavy. Much like a house, a reef needs to be built on a solid foundation. The Great Barrier Reef, for example, is built on the shallow ocean floor off Australia's coast. The Maldives are nowhere near a shallow coast. Instead, the foundation of the atolls is an underwater chain of volcanoes.

Turquoise coral islands rise out of the Indian Ocean like gemstones in a view of the Maldives from the air.

INDIA

SRI LANKA

Minicoy I.
(India)

Eight Degree Channel

Laccadive Sea

N

Ihavandiffulu Atoll

Tiladummati Atoll

Makunudu Atoll

Miladummadulu Atoll

Malosmadulu Atoll

Fadiffolu Atoll

Indian Ocean

MALDIVES

Kardiva Channel

Male Atoll

Male Island

Ari Atoll

South Male Atoll

Felidu Atoll

Nilandu
Atoll

Mulaka Atoll

Kolumadulu Atoll

Haddummati Atoll

One and Half Degree Channel

Suvadiva Atoll

Equatorial Channel

Addu Atoll

Gan Island

0	100	200 Miles
0	100	200	300 Kilometers

Dunidu I.

Hulele
Island

AIR STRIP

Funadu I.

Male Passage

Wilingili
Island

Male ✪

8 ft (2.4 m)

Male
Island

Rat
Point

Wild
Point

Wadu Channel

0	1	2 Miles
0	1	2 Kilometers

The Maldives is a country made entirely of about 1,200 coral islands that barely rise above sea level in the Indian Ocean. The islands are clustered into several formations called atolls.

23

Rings of Coral

An atoll is a circular ring of coral in the open sea, built up on a sunken bank, or formed on the crater of a volcano that has sunk below the surface of the sea.

FORMATION OF AN ATOLL

THE BEGINNING OF AN ATOLL
The undersea flanks of an ocean volcano are colonized by corals, which continue to grow.

Volcanic cone · Coral reef · Inactive volcano

THE CORALS GAIN GROUND
As the surrounding reef settles and continues to expand, it becomes a barrier reef that surrounds the summit of the ancient volcano, now inactive.

Coral reef · Inactive volcano

THE ATOLL SOLIDIFIES
Eventually the volcano will be worn down by waves and sink below the water, leaving a ring of growing coral with a shallow lagoon in the middle.

Coral reef forms a ring · Inactive volcano

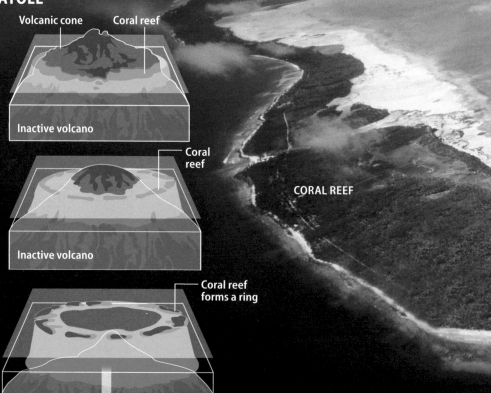

CORAL REEF

WHAT ARE CORALS

Reef-building corals live together in colonies. A single member of the colony, called a *polyp*, has a cylinder-shaped body. Its mouth lies at the top of the body, and tiny tentacles surround the mouth. The polyps remove minerals from ocean water to form their skeletons. Only the top layer is living coral. Coral skeletons accumulate and branch out over time on top of older dead corals to create a reef.

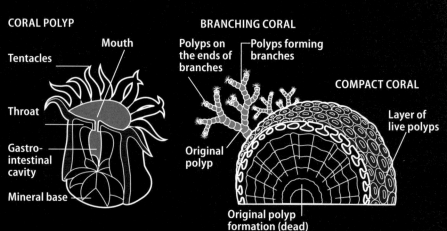

CORAL POLYP
Mouth · Tentacles · Throat · Gastro-intestinal cavity · Mineral base

BRANCHING CORAL
Polyps on the ends of branches · Polyps forming branches · Original polyp

COMPACT CORAL
Layer of live polyps · Original polyp formation (dead)

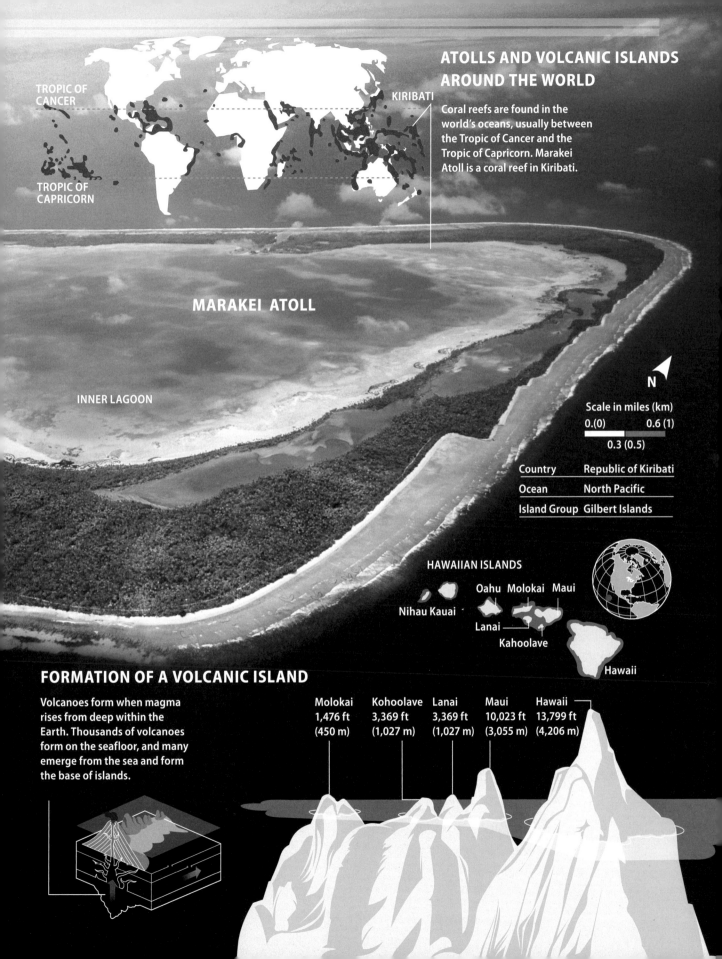

ATOLLS AND VOLCANIC ISLANDS AROUND THE WORLD

TROPIC OF CANCER

TROPIC OF CAPRICORN

KIRIBATI

Coral reefs are found in the world's oceans, usually between the Tropic of Cancer and the Tropic of Capricorn. Marakei Atoll is a coral reef in Kiribati.

MARAKEI ATOLL

INNER LAGOON

N

Scale in miles (km)
0.(0)   0.6 (1)
          0.3 (0.5)

Country	Republic of Kiribati
Ocean	North Pacific
Island Group	Gilbert Islands

HAWAIIAN ISLANDS

Oahu Molokai Maui
Nihau Kauai
Lanai
Kahoolave
Hawaii

FORMATION OF A VOLCANIC ISLAND

Volcanoes form when magma rises from deep within the Earth. Thousands of volcanoes form on the seafloor, and many emerge from the sea and form the base of islands.

Molokai 1,476 ft (450 m)	Kohoolave 3,369 ft (1,027 m)	Lanai 3,369 ft (1,027 m)	Maui 10,023 ft (3,055 m)	Hawaii 13,799 ft (4,206 m)

A Sinking Feeling

Many islands are the tops of volcanic mountains that lie mostly underwater. The Maldives' mountaintops are completely beneath the sea, but the coral structures built on top of them rise above the waves—just barely, though.

How did mountains end up in the middle of the ocean? Earth's **crust**—including the ocean floor—floats on a sea of hot, molten rock called **magma.** Volcanoes are born when this magma flows up through gaps in the crust, cools, and turns into solid mountains.

About 350,000 people live in the Maldives. Most are descendants of people from Sri Lanka, a large island off the coast of India. Living on a chain of volcanoes might seem stressful. But none of the volcanoes beneath the Maldives is active or dangerous. In addition, the surrounding coral **reefs** act as shields, protecting the low-lying islands from storms and high waves.

The main danger to the islands comes from **global warming.** As Earth warms, the polar ice caps melt, causing the sea level to rise. Also, warm water itself expands, filling up slightly more space than cold, which also makes the seas higher.

The low-lying Maldives islands are seriously threatened by rising sea levels. Some scientists predict that the ocean could cover most of the Maldives as soon as 2100.

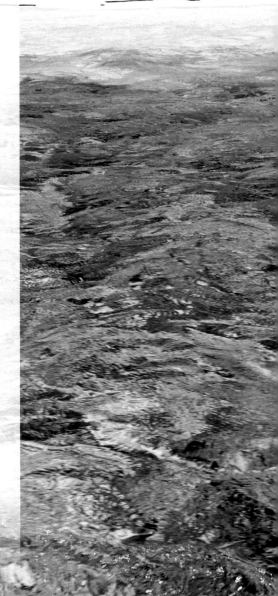

The islands that make up the Maldives barely rise above the surrounding ocean. Coral reefs around them help protect the islands from storms and waves.

The Mid-Atlantic Ridge

Where Is the Mid-Atlantic Ridge and What's Special About It?

The Mid-Atlantic Ridge is a gigantic mountain range that lies almost completely underwater. The range runs down the middle of the entire Atlantic Ocean, from Iceland toward Antarctica, like a planet-sized zipper.

What exactly is being unzipped here? The answer is Earth's **crust,** made of solid rock. This outer layer is actually made up of several rigid slabs, thick areas, that "float" on a layer of rock below that is so hot it flows. Their motion is described by the theory of **plate tectonics.** The slabs are called tectonic plates.

Earth's tectonic plates are moving very slowly relative to one another. They move at speeds up to about 4 inches (10 centimeters) per year. Some plates are pulling apart while others are colliding. Over millions of years, these plates move great distances.

In the middle of the Atlantic Ocean, some of Earth's tectonic plates are spreading apart. **Magma**—molten rock—shoots up through the "unzipped" gap between the plates. Ocean water quickly cools the magma. It turns from liquid magma to solid mountains. The same process forms volcanoes, including the island bases of the Maldives located in the Indian Ocean. In fact, the Mid-Atlantic Ridge is really a gigantic chain of underwater volcanoes!

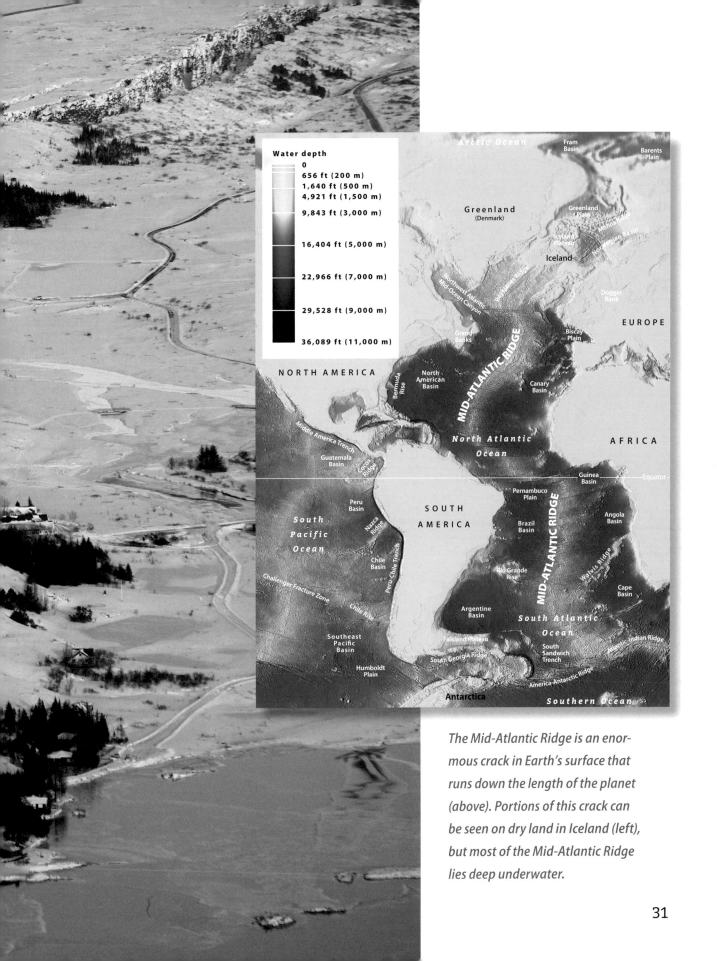

Water depth

	0
	656 ft (200 m)
	1,640 ft (500 m)
	4,921 ft (1,500 m)
	9,843 ft (3,000 m)
	16,404 ft (5,000 m)
	22,966 ft (7,000 m)
	29,528 ft (9,000 m)
	36,089 ft (11,000 m)

The Mid-Atlantic Ridge is an enormous crack in Earth's surface that runs down the length of the planet (above). Portions of this crack can be seen on dry land in Iceland (left), but most of the Mid-Atlantic Ridge lies deep underwater.

31

Mountains in the Dark

Only a few parts of the Mid-Atlantic Ridge rise above the ocean's surface, forming islands. Iceland is the biggest island that is crossed directly by the Mid-Atlantic Ridge. A few scattered islands in the middle of the Atlantic Ocean, including the Azores and Ascension Island, are also part of the Mid-Atlantic Ridge.

The rest of the mountain range lies deep beneath the waves. The ridge is bordered on the east and west by broad, flat *abyssal plains.* The word *abyss* means *great depth.* These featureless plains lie 14,000 to 18,000 feet (4,300 to 5,500 meters) below sea level. They extend west toward the Americas and east toward Europe and Africa.

Most of the Mid-Atlantic Ridge rises no more than 10,000 feet (3,000 meters) above the surrounding abyssal plains. Thus, the mountaintops are still submerged beneath thousands of feet or meters of water. No sunlight can reach such depths. The water is cold, silent, and appears black. The great weight of the ocean above presses down, creating crushing pressure.

Perhaps more than any other environment on Earth, the ocean depths are completely hostile to human life. And without sunlight, plants and algae cannot use **photosynthesis** to survive. For many years, scientists assumed that the ocean depths were lifeless. They certainly never expected to find an explosion of **biodiversity** around the Mid-Atlantic Ridge.

A diver explores a section of the Mid-Atlantic Ridge offshore near Iceland. However, most of the ridge lies underwater at depths too great for divers to reach.

EXPLORING THE RIDGE

Scientists have explored the Mid-Atlantic Ridge with vehicles called *submersibles*. A submersible has thick metal walls that can withstand the great pressure beneath the sea. In 1974, the American explorer Robert Duane Ballard led the first expedition to see the ridge up close with submersibles, called Project FAMOUS (French-American Mid-Ocean Undersea Study).

Robert Ballard explored the Mid-Atlantic Ridge in a submersible (above), named Alvin, that was launched from a support ship with the help of a large crane.

The Lost City

The ancient Greek philosopher Plato wrote about a continent called Atlantis. According to legend, an advanced civilization lived on Atlantis, before it sank beneath the ocean and vanished.

The Atlantis Massif is a dome-shaped underwater mountain just west of the Mid-Atlantic Ridge. Scientists named the mountain in reference to the legendary Atlantis. But they did not find the remnants of a human civilization on top of it. Instead, in 2000, they found something much stranger: a place they called the "Lost City."

The Lost City is built from **hydrothermal vents.** At such vents, hot, mineral-rich water flows up from cracks in the rock. The water quickly cools, and the minerals stick together, forming large chimneylike structures.

Many strange creatures make their home around the Lost City. Some are **invertebrates,** such as crabs, sea urchins, and even some corals **adapted** to live in the depths. But the most important living things in the Lost City are microbes. These microbes make food from chemicals in the hot water flowing from the vents. Other creatures eat these microbes.

Many other hydrothermal vents along the Mid-Atlantic Ridge are heated by **magma** near the surface. Hot, mineral-rich black water turns black as it flows from the vents and cools. It looks like smoke from a chimney. These "black smokers" support a diverse community of strange creatures.

An enormous underwater mountain just west of the Mid-Atlantic Ridge, seen in this false-color radar image (right), was named the Atlantis Massif by scientists after the sunken continent from ancient Greek legend. The word massif *refers to a mountain.*

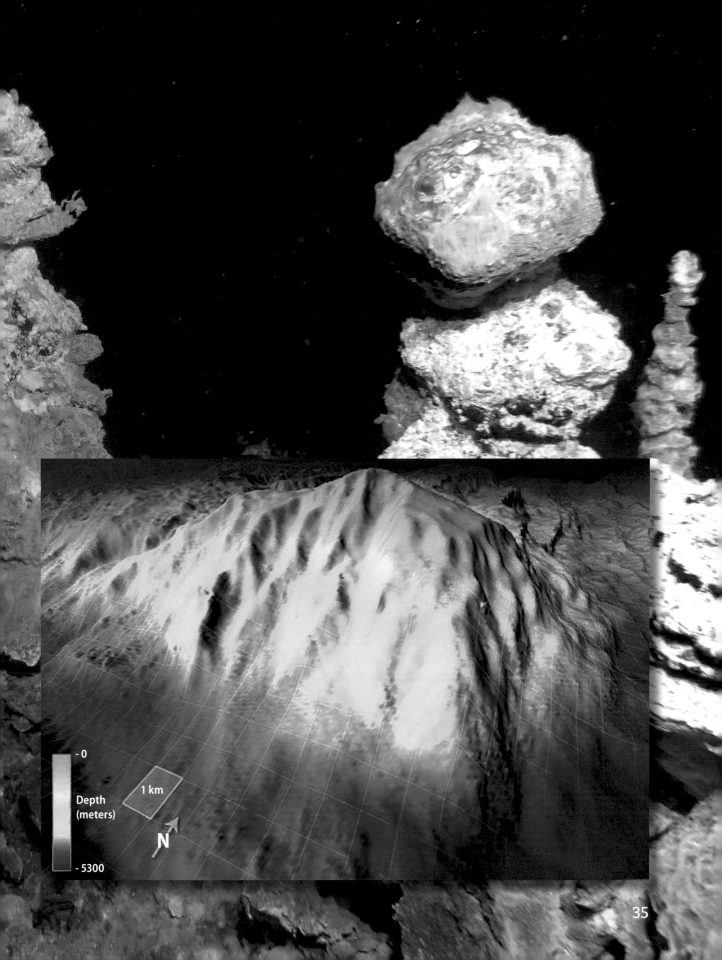

- 0

Depth
(meters)

1 km

N

- 5300

The Lost City

continued from previous page

But the Lost City is different from most hydrothermal vents. The Atlantis Massif is an unusual mountain made of a greenish rock, peridotite (*PEHR uh DOH tyt*), that is usually found deep beneath Earth's **crust.** Because of the action of **plate tectonics** along the Mid-Atlantic Ridge, a mass of peridotite rose up through the crust, forming the mountain.

Minerals in seawater react with the rock to generate heat. The reaction also provides chemicals that microbes use to make food. These microbes are **extremophiles,** meaning they can survive in a place that would kill almost any other kind of life.

The nature of these extremophiles may prove to be one of the greatest of all the treasures of the ocean. They are a clue to solving the mystery of life itself. Scientists know that early life forms on Earth did not get food from **photosynthesis.** They have long wondered if the first life forms got food from chemical reactions in hydrothermal vents. The unique chemistry of the Lost City may help us learn how life on Earth began.

The floor of the Atlantis Massif (left) supports a community of strange creatures that live without sunlight.

Hot mineral-rich water pours from a hydrothermal vent at the Lost City (below left) along the Mid-Atlantic Ridge. Microbes use the chemicals to make food other animals then eat the microbes.

THE MINOANS: A REAL-LIFE ATLANTIS?

Scientists and scholars think the legend of Atlantis may contain a bit of truth. Hundreds of years before Plato's time, the advanced Minoan civilization lived on islands near Greece. Around 1470 B.C., volcanic eruptions destroyed the Minoan island of Thira, along with much of the Minoan's civilization. **Plate tectonics** may have destroyed the "real" Atlantis, even as it helped form the Lost City!

A decorated stone wall (above) is one of few remains of the Minoan civilization on the Greek island of Knossos. The Minoans may have inspired the legend of Atlantis.

Glossary

adapt when living things change to survive in their surroundings

algae a group of simple plantlike organisms that can make their own food

atoll a ring of coral in the open ocean, often built up around an underwater volcano

biodiversity variety of living things that live in the same place

colony a group of corals or other animals that live close together in a single structure

coral a jellyfishlike animal that builds limestone "skeletons," forming reefs

crust the outer layer of Earth, made of solid rock

extremophile a living thing, usually microscopic, that thrives in conditions deadly to most other life

global warming a rise in Earth's average temperature, largely due to human activity since the mid-1800's

hydrothermal vent an opening in the seafloor through which hot, mineral-rich water flows up

invertebrate an animal without a backbone

limestone a rock made of calcium carbonate that forms coral reefs

magma molten (hot liquid) rock beneath Earth's crust that flows up through cracks, forming volcanoes

nutrients nourishing substances, such as minerals dissolved in water, that living things need

plate tectonics a scientific idea that describes the gradual motion of about 30 immense areas called plates covering Earth's surface

photosynthesis a process used by plants and some algae to make food from sunlight.

polyp a wormlike form of certain animals, such as corals, that usually stays rooted to one place

reef a rock formation just under the ocean surface, often made from coral

symbiosis a close relationship between two living things. In *mutualism*, both benefit from the relationship

zooxanthellae algae that live inside the bodies of corals

Find Out More

Where Is the Great Barrier Reef (Where is...?) by Nico Medina and John Hinderliter (Penguin Random House , 2016) *Read this book to continue exploring the Great Barrier Reef!*

Ocean: A Visual Encyclopedia by John Woodward (DK Publishing, 2015) *A visual encyclopedia that contains facts and photography to teach kids about ocean life.*

Atlantic Ocean by Louise Spilsbury and Richard Spilsbury (London Raintree, 2015) *Young readers can read maps about places, islands, and busy ports on the Atlantic. They will also learn more about the weather and explore the ocean floor.*

Use Your Noodle!

In this book, you've learned about two ways in which ocean landforms are created. Corals make the first kind of landform—**limestone** reefs—from minerals dissolved in water. The second kind of landform—mountain ridges—forms from magma that erupts through gaps in Earth's **crust.** Do you think similar processes made rocks and other landforms found on dry land? Perhaps you've seen such landforms near your home. Describe what you've seen and how those landforms might have been created.

Acknowledgments

Cover © Flip Nicklin, Minden Pictures/ National Geographic Creative

4-5 © Shutterstock

6-7 © Flip Nicklin, Minden Pictures/ National Geographic Creative

8-9 © Shutterstock

10-11 © redbrickstock.com/Alamy Images

12-13 © Oliver Lucanus, NiS/Minden Pictures/SuperStock; © Marcos Amend, Shutterstock

14-15 © Angela N Perryman, Shutterstock; © Jim Lopes, Shutterstock; © Fred Kamphues, Shutterstock; © iStock; © imageBROKER/Alamy Images

16-17 © Shutterstock; © Mark Conlin, SuperStock; © Andrii Slonchak, Shutterstock; © Norbert Wu, SuperStock; © Stephan Kerkhofs, Shutterstock

18-19 © Ron and Valerie Taylor, ardea.c/ Pantheon/SuperStock

20-21 © imageBROKER/Alamy Images

22-23 © Shutterstock

24-25 © Sol 90 Images

26-27 © imageBROKER/Alamy Images; © Shutterstock

28-29 © imageBROKER/Alamy Images

30-31 © Arctic Images/Alamy Images

32-33 © Poelzer Wolfgang, Alamy Images; © AP Photo

34-35 © R.B. Pedersen, University of Bergen; © University of Washington

36-37 © Ralph White, Getty Images; IFE, URI-IAO, UW, Lost City Science Party/NOAA/OAR/OER/The Lost City 2005 Expedition; © Ralf Siemieniec, Shutterstock

Index